Our pets aren't just animals; they are members of our family. As such, when they become ill, we want to ease their pain. But this attitude of dogs as family members is actually a fairly recent attitude shift and, as a result of that, there's still a lot of mystery surrounding caring for old dogs.

It wasn't until the 1990s that spaying and neutering became a standard practice in the wellness care of our dogs. Since then we've begun to provide our dogs with routine visits to the vet which result in better health. The food we feed them is more nutritional and we even invest in grooming our dogs which has positive health benefits as well. All of this, and the fact that more dogs now live indoors, away from nature's bad weather, leads to our dogs living longer.

In their senior years, our loyal dogs are suffering many of the same geriatric diseases that people suffer from. But many of us have never experienced a pet in these advanced years because dogs are living so much longer than perhaps our last pet did.

I even see a tremendous difference between three years ago, when my Golden Retriever Jake was euthanized, and today. I don't know if it's because I'm more educated today then I was then – or if there is more information for dog owners now than there was back then.

I do know if I knew then what I know now, I would have done a few things differently. First of all I would have considered a harness to help Jake stand and squat. I don't know if this would have extended his life, but it would have made his last few months a bit more comfortable when his arthritis and hip dysplasia was taking its toll on him.

They didn't have a drug for his Cognitive Dysfunction – or if they did my vet didn't yet know about it. But if they'd have had it, I would have tried it. I felt so sorry for him when he began suffering from memory loss. On occasion I could see that he didn't know where his food or water bowl was or which door to go to to go outside.

And more than anything, if there had been in-home euthanasia, I absolutely would have gone that route. Jake's last moments were spent on a cold vet floor, with me lying next to him; cuddling him, petting him and telling him how much I loved him. When we went to the vet she laid a blanket down for him to lie on. But with his paws he pushed it aside to lie on the cold tile floor. I lay on the floor with him, my arm over his chest as the vet administered the meds that would end Jake's life – and his suffering. I sobbed. Even after he was gone, I lay with him and cried.

That was over three years ago and even as I recount this; tears are welling up in my eyes. But it was through this experience that I came to want to know more about the afflictions that our old pals face. I started with the diseases that Jake suffered from, which led to curiosity about other health issues for senior dogs.

When I was going through this with Jake, I didn't know where to turn – other than my vet. And as good of a doctor as she was, I needed to understand in non-medical terms what happens to a senior dog. And her answers only gave me more questions.

This book is a compilation of what I've learned about the most common health afflictions that old dogs suffer from.

It is certainly not intended to be a *replacement* for veterinary advice, but rather a supplement.

If you are reading this book, I'm sure it's because you have a senior dog you care for deeply that is suffering from something. My heart goes out to you. I hope the information provided here is of benefit to you as you comfort your buddy through this period of life.

I dedicate this book to my old pal Jake, my good friend Jim who encouraged me to write this, to all old dogs who have brought and continue to bring joy to their humans and to every person who knows the pure love of a faithful dog. Lastly, I dedicate this book to my young Bulldog, Jes who brings me so much happiness. One day I will have to say good bye to her as well, but for now, I cherish every lick and cuddle she offers me.

Contents

- Obesity 7
- Degenerative Myelopathy 11
- Inflammatory Bowel Disease 15
- Epilepsy 19
- Cognitive Dysfunction (Dog Alzheimer) 23
- Cancer 27
- Prostate Problems 32
- Urinary Incontinence 36
- Chronic Valvular Disease 39
- Cardiomyopathy 43
- Hypothyroidism 47
- Cushing's Disease 51
- Kidney Disease 55
- Glaucoma 59
- Cataracts 62
- Arthritis 66
- Dental Disease and Gingivitis 71

Obesity

A chubby puppy may look adorable, but the same can't be said for older dogs. Not that older dogs look ugly when they put on too much weight. It's just that any excess pounds are unhealthy. Obesity is one of the main health problems in older dogs and leads to other health problems as well. It's estimated that one-out-of-every-four dogs in the U.S. is obese.

A dog is considered obese if he weighs 20% or more above the ideal body weight. A simple test to determine if your dog is obese is to place your hands on your dog's rib cage. Ideally you should be able to feel his ribs easily as well as detect an observable waist. If you do, congratulations! Your furry friend is in his proper weight. However, if you're unable to detect even a slight hint of a rib cage on your pooch, much less a defined waist, then your dog is likely to be obese.

There are several causes of obesity in older dogs. One contributor is breed. Breeds that are predisposed to obesity include Golden Retrievers, Labrador Retrievers,

Dachshunds, Shelties, Basset Hounds, Beagles, Cocker Spaniels and Cairn Terriers.

Metabolic disorders also contribute to too much weight, but these are rare. More often than not, canine obesity results from feeding your old dog too much and not giving him enough opportunity to exercise. Obesity is the most common nutritional disorder in dogs today – and it's the most controllable. It's up to YOU to understand the appropriate amount of food to feed your dog, and to stick to those recommendations. Your dog may eat more than usual because he's bored, greedy, or used to overeating. Giving into these her begging is NOT a demonstration of love. Caring for her health is the way to show your dog you love her.

As dogs age, their metabolism slows down and their food needs change. Ask your vet what your dog's ideal weight should be and work towards that number. Don't starve your pooch to get there. Don't put her on a "diet" but make a "lifestyle change."

1. Consider what food you are feeding your dog. It may be time to change to a "senior" food or a "light" food. But beware: just because the packaging says "light" doesn't mean it's the formula your dog needs. It may only be lighter than the same brand's non-light variety.

2. If your dog is tremendously obese, you may ask your vet for a special food that you need a prescription to purchase.

3. Consider feeding your dog smaller portions five times a day instead of one or two larger meals.

4. If your dog is used to begging for food at the table, and you're used to feeding table scraps to him during a meal, keep your dog out of the room the next time you sit for a meal.

5. Be sure your dog doesn't lose weight too quickly. This will have a negative impact on her overall health.

6. Add exercise to your old dog's daily routine. If your dog hasn't been exercising, start slowly. A 5-minute stroll is plenty to start with and you can build up from there. Set a goal to eventually work up to a 20 minute walk. You might also consider taking your dog to an indoor canine swimming center. Swimming is great exercise for obese dogs. It's said that five minutes of swimming is the equivalent of a 20-minute walk.

As our dogs get older we begin to acknowledge that they won't be with us for many more years. There are many health issues we simply have to accept. But the one thing we can fully control to help our pooches live longer is to manage their weight through proper diet and exercise.

Degenerative Myelopathy

Degenerative myelopathy is a rare, progressive disease that attacks the spinal cord of the affected canine. The disease is one of the leading causes of limb weakness, lameness, and paralysis in older dogs; particularly those between eight and fourteen years old. As the name implies, degenerative myelopathy becomes worse as it progresses. The specific cause for the disorder isn't known, but experts suspect a genetic factor could play a significant part.

Degenerative myelopathy occurs when the protective tissue covering the spinal neurons (called myelin sheath) begins to disintegrate. This deterioration causes the axons, the nerve fibers underneath, to degenerate. When the axons fall apart, the communication lines between the brain and the spinal cord don't work.

The signs and symptoms of degenerative myelopathy in older dogs begin with ataxia, wherein loss of muscle coordination is seen. The disorder strikes a dog's hind limbs first, and one hind limb is usually affected before the other. Muscle weakness is one of the first noticeable signs. Other signs include:

- Lameness
- Balance problems
- Incontinence
- Rear-paw dragging
- Paralysis
- Difficulty moving about (e.g., walking, running, or jumping)
- Worn toenails
- Sores on paws

Large, purebred canines are at a higher risk for acquiring degenerative myelopathy when they grow older. German Shepherds are most often diagnosed with the disease. Degenerative myelopathy also affects Irish Setters, Rhodesian Ridgebacks, Boxers, Collies, and Standard Poodles. The disorder equally affects male and female dogs. Degenerative myelopathy is generally an old dog disease but in rare occasions the disease strikes a younger dog.

Degenerative myelopathy is difficult to diagnose. The disease is of a rule-out kind. This means that the vet only comes to the conclusion that degenerative myelopathy is indeed the cause behind your old dog's signs and symptoms *after* the other disorders that also cause paralysis have been ruled out. The vet conducts a series of neurological tests on your pooch. A urinalysis, complete blood count, and radiographs are also used to determine degenerative myelopathy. Sadly, degenerative myelopathy in older dogs is only diagnosed reliably in postmortem when the dog's spinal cord is examined microscopically.

There is presently no cure for degenerative myelopathy in canines. However, with your vet's help, there are ways that can be done to improve the quality of your dog's life and put off the progression of the disorder.

Supportive care, exercise, and physical therapy are the best treatments for canines riddled with degenerative myelopathy. Consider purchasing a cart or harness to help your dog walk. If your dog is no longer able to walk, turn him at regular intervals to prevent pressure sores from forming. Groom her regularly and make sure to keep his bed clean and dry. Because movement is difficult, dogs with degenerative myelopathy tend to gain weight. Changing your dog's diet so he doesn't gain weight is recommended.

Unfortunately the prognosis for older dogs with degenerative myelopathy isn't bright, but there's no agreed-upon timeframe as to the average amount of time you can expect your pooch to continue to live. Some experts say as little as six months while others say as long as two+ years.

If you suspect your dog has degenerative myelopathy, of course you must visit your vet, but also visit this website: http://mydoghasdm.com. It is both a wealth of information and a tremendous support group of people with dogs with degenerative myelopathy.

Inflammatory Bowel Disease

Gastrointestinal (GI) disorders are one of the many conditions that make their presence felt in dogs who are in their senior years. One of the more common afflictions is inflammatory bowel disease. Also known as IBD, the disease refers to a cluster of GI disorders wherein the gastrointestinal tract is invaded by white blood cells, or inflammatory cells. The disease attacks both the upper and lower gastrointestinal tracts, which are the stomach and small intestine and colon, respectively. The cause of IBD is unknown, but the disorder is responsible for the majority of long-term diarrhea and vomiting incidents in dogs.

While IBD is mostly seen in older dogs, it can also strike in younger dogs. Certain breeds have a higher risk for acquiring inflammatory bowel disease:
- Boxer
- German Shepherd
- Rottweiler
- Shar–Pei
- Soft-coated Wheaton Terrier

The signs and symptoms of IBD depend on the gastrointestinal organ affected. However, there are a couple of telltale signs that could suggest your old dog is suffering from IBD. Vomiting and diarrhea are the two most common signs indicating IBD. Vomiting indicates a problem in the small intestine and stomach while diarrhea suggests the problem is in the large intestine. Vomiting and diarrhea can appear either together or separately. The signs may also be intermittent, but for the whole duration, the dog's condition worsens and your pooch will undoubtedly lose his appetite.

Signs that point to inflammatory bowel disease in older dogs:

- Weight loss
- Energy loss
- Decreased energy levels
- Depression
- Low-grade fever
- Swollen abdomen
- Loose, watery stools
- Mucus in stools
- Gas

If your pooch suffers from the symptoms above, take him to the vet as soon as possible. Your vet will perform a series of non-invasive tests including a urinalysis, blood panel, radiograph, and broad-spectrum deworming. If these tests don't reveal conclusive results for IBD, the vet will then conduct a biopsy either through surgery or an endoscopy.

The treatment for IBD is focused on reducing the inflammation present in the intestines and to stop the symptoms from occurring again. Medications like corticosteroids, loperamide, bismuth subsalicylate, and metronidazole are common medicines recommended by vets for cases of IBD. Dietary changes are also helpful in keeping the disorder in check.

Once your old pooch has been diagnosed with IBD, don't expect immediate results, and don't get frustrated when you don't see any. It takes quite a while to find the right combination of medicine and diet to combat inflammatory bowel disease in older dogs. Don't give up during the "trial and error" period because once you and your vet find the right combination you're old dog, and you, will be much happier.

Epilepsy

Regardless of age, any dog can be afflicted with epilepsy but older dogs are more susceptible to the disease because of the changes that are taking place in their brains.

Epilepsy is a disorder of the brain. It causes dogs to have uncontrollable, sudden physical attacks that may also be called a convulsion, fit, or seizure. Epilepsy in older dogs is a frightening experience especially for those who see it happening for the first time. Seeing your buddy shaking, stiff, either conscious or unconscious, and foaming at the mouth can cause panic. But when you see your older dog experiencing a fit, the best thing you can do is remain calm and wait for the episode to be over. Seizures generally last between 30 seconds and a minute-and-a-half.

Epilepsy is due to either idiopathic (unknown) reasons or genetic abnormalities. The former is more common than the latter. Although the cause behind idiopathic epilepsy is unknown, studies reveal that brain lesions are present in a dog suffering from epilepsy. Male dogs are more likely to suffer from epilepsy than female dogs. Unless medical attention is given, idiopathic epilepsy attacks may occur more frequently and become more severe after every attack.

Breeds that are predisposed to idiopathic epilepsy are Beagle, Belgian Tervuren, Keeshond, Golden and Labrador Retrievers, Shetland Sheepdog and Vizsla.

Epilepsy due to genetic abnormalities, on the other hand, can appear in dogs as early as six months old. An example of a genetic abnormality that can cause epilepsy in canines is hydrocephalus, also referred to as "water in the brain."

Two factors are considered in the diagnosis of epilepsy in older dogs: the age at which the dog experienced her first epileptic seizure and the epilepsy pattern, specifically the type and frequency. To determine if your old dog has epilepsy, your vet will conduct a physical examination, consider your dog's medical history, run blood tests and a urinalysis. Brain scans, like a computed tomography (CT) scan and magnetic resonance imaging (MRI) are also helpful methods that can provide useful information.

Once the cause for the epilepsy has been determined, the vet will then take measures to control the main cause for the disorder so as to reduce the chances of the epileptic seizures from happening again. Epilepsy in older dogs is often controlled through anticonvulsant drugs prescribed by the vet. Phenobarbital and primidone are two of the most popular drugs prescribed for dogs with epilepsy.

If your old dog is diagnosed with epilepsy and placed on medication to control seizures, there are several elements for you to consider:

- Don't let your dog swim. She could drown if she has a seizure while in the water.
- Most seizures occur at night or early morning, when the dog is resting.
- Epileptic drugs often cause weight gain. Be sure to monitor your dog's weight and, if necessary, adjust her diet and exercise so she doesn't develop weight problem.
- Follow your vet's directions carefully. Be sure to take your dog to the vet as routinely scheduled to monitor medications in his blood stream. And be sure to NOT stop giving your dog his meds. Dogs

must be weaned off of drugs for epilepsy. Stopping abruptly can cause increased health problems for your dog.

Though epilepsy in older dogs cannot be prevented, just like epilepsy in people, it can be managed.

If your dog has experienced a seizure, consult your vet immediately. Additionally, a website you'll likely find helpful is: http://www.canine-seizures.freeservers.com

Cognitive Dysfunction (Dog Alzheimer)

Cognitive dysfunction in older dogs, also known as cognitive dysfunction syndrome (CDS), used to be known as the old-dog syndrome or senile-dog syndrome. This illness is similar to Alzheimer's in people in the sense that the brain of the affected dog goes through several changes that result in the rapid decline of the dog's mental abilities. Thinking, learned behavior, memory, and recognition are some of the mental faculties affected by the disease, which affects more than 50% of dogs who are ten+ years old. As with most health conditions in older dogs, the illness is progressive, meaning it worsens with age.

When old dogs begin to show strange, unusual behavior—like suddenly appearing to be lost and confused inside the house, for instance—most dog owners attribute the behavior to simply getting old. However, cognitive dysfunction in older dogs is something that needs to be taken seriously. If the disease is ignored and medical intervention is put off, your pooch's condition could become worse, and since his mental faculties are no longer performing the way they should be, he is at high risk for getting hurt.

Signs and symptoms of cognitive dysfunction can be tough to spot, so here are some things to watch for in your older dog. Assuming your dog isn't ill with cancer or other age-related diseases, he could be suffering from cognitive dysfunction should these signs be present:

Disorientation

Disorientation is one of the main symptoms in cognitive dysfunction in older dogs. Signs of disorientation include when he gets lost inside the house or in the yard, has a tough time finding the door, no longer recognizes familiar people, and doesn't answer to his name or verbal cues.

Changes in sleep and activity patterns

Watch out for sudden changes in your dog's sleep and activity patterns. He could be sleeping way too much in a 24-hour period but not get enough sleep at night. Purposeful activity decreases while restlessness and aimless activity increase.

Soiling the house

Your dog may be the best house-trained canine in the world, but when cognitive dysfunction enters the scene, all that training goes out the window. Your dog may not signal as much to go outside. Peeing and pooping indoors start happening more and more frequently.

Other Signs

- Withdrawing from interacting with you, including asking for less petting and attention
- Staring at walls or into space or wandering aimlessly
- Getting "stuck" in familiar places, like in corners or behind furniture
- Not recognizing family members or other familiar people

There is no specific method to test cognitive dysfunction in senior canines. Veterinarians make the diagnosis only when underlying diseases have been ruled out and according to the severity and number of signs present in the dog. Diseases your vet will rule out include hypothyroidism, kidney problems, arthritis, and hearing and vision loss.

There's also no cure. But according to the *American Animal Hospital Association (AAHA)*, "… there is increasing hope. There is now a prescription drug available to treat dogs with CDS in the US (two are available in Europe). It works by increasing the amount of dopamine in the dog's brain. Dopamine is a neurotransmitter that the brain needs to function normally; an increased amount of dopamine can improve brain function. Though it doesn't work in all dogs, the drug can help many dogs with CDS think more clearly, remember more, return to their interactions with family, and enjoy a higher quality of life in their elderly years." **That drug is Anipryl (selegiline), a drug used by humans to combat Parkinson's disease.**

Cancer

Hearing the word *cancer* is enough to strike fear in the hearts of most people. Cancer in older dogs is very widespread, affecting one out of every three dogs, and is the #1 cause of death in dogs today. Of course, with the vast improvement of science and technology, the dogs today are living longer than their counterparts from decades ago. Unfortunately, even the latest and most sophisticated discovery in the medical world is not enough to prevent any dog from getting the dreaded "Big C."

Older dogs are more prone to getting cancer because of the decrease in performance of their body systems and functions, but as with other diseases, certain breeds seem to be more susceptible to certain types of cancer.

The five most common canine cancers include:

Lymphoma, also called lymphosarcoma, is a very aggressive cancer of the lymph tissue and is the most frequently treated canine cancer. Caught early enough it can be treated but if it diagnosed in the latter stage, it is most often fatal.

Osteosarcoma is the most common canine bone cancer and usually affects large and giant breed dogs. This cancer is also aggressive, usually requires amputation and chemotherapy.

Soft tissue sarcomas affect soft tissues like fat, muscle, nerves, fibrous tissues, blood vessels, and deep skin tissues. They can be found in any part of the body. Most of them develop in the arms or legs but they can be found anywhere in the body, including internal organs. This type of cancer is generally treated surgically. There are many different types of soft tissue cancers. Following are some of them and the breed that is most at risk for the particular type of soft tissue cancer.

- Shetland Sheepdog – Liposarcoma
- Basset Hound – Trichoepithelioma
- Kerry Blue Terrier – Pilomatricoma
- Cocker Spaniel – Cutaneous Plasmacytoma

Mast cell tumors (MCTs) appear on the skin and unless they are treated immediately can become malignant and spread. They may be treated through surgery, radiation, chemotherapy or steroids. Which treatment depends on the stage of the tumor. Boxers and Pugs are high-risk breeds for MCT.

Hemangiosarcoma tends to attack the heart, liver, spleen and skin, but it can spread anywhere. It is usually diagnosed via a biopsy and though it cannot be cured, it can be treated in an effort to control this cancer from spreading.

Mouth Cancer affects the mouth and throat and is generally identified via x-ray or CT scan and biopsied to determine the type and extent of the cancer. Treatment generally requires surgery and sometimes radiation.

Breast Cancer in dogs is three times more common that breast cancer in people and it tends to occur more in female dogs who have not been spayed. Obese dogs also suffer breast cancer more than dogs that are fit. If caught early enough the cancer can often be surgically removed. Sometime chemotherapy is also recommended.

Toy and Miniature Poodles, English Springer Spaniels, Pointers and German Shepherds are reportedly at greater risk than other breeds.

It can be tricky to spot the signs and symptoms of cancer, particularly in older dogs, because signs of cancer in older dogs mimic the symptoms that also point to the aging process, such as weight loss, energy loss or lethargy, and lameness. Because there are different kinds of cancer, the symptoms may vary depending on the type.

Yet there are red flags that appear in almost every type of cancer. You should be on the lookout if your old dog displays:

- Unusual swelling
- Abnormal bleeding or discharge
- Sores that do not heal
- Behavioral changes
- Breathing difficulties
- Bowel-moving difficulties

If your old dog is exhibiting any of the signs presented above, it's best to make that trip to the vet. The vet will perform the necessary physical examinations and conduct laboratory tests to confirm if your old dog does have cancer. Cancer in older dogs may sound like a death sentence for your pooch, but this isn't necessarily the case. In cancer, early detection is a significant factor for cure.

The earlier your dog's cancer is detected and treated, the better. If you catch the cancer before it spreads, you're more like to cure it through surgery, chemotherapy, radiation therapy, immunotherapy, or a combination of these. If, however, the cancer has spread, it is less likely that your vet will be able to cure your pooch.

Prostate Problems

Prostate problems are more likely to occur in older dogs who were not neutered in their younger years. For neutered canines, the risk of acquiring prostate problems is significantly lower. This is due to the prostate either not developing at all or dwindling to a smaller size depending on the age at which your dog was neutered. Still, castration does not guarantee complete protection from the development of prostate problems.

Present only in male dogs, the prostate gland is more of an accessory sex gland, releasing a fluid that gives off nutrients and facilitates the sperm's movements.

The signs of prostate problems in older dogs begin to show up when a dog reaches six years. Here are the three most common prostate problems plaguing dogs. Regardless of their severity, these problems should be given due medical attention to prevent complications in the long run:

Benign prostatic hyperplasia, or BPH, is the most common prostate problem encountered by non-neutered canines.

Also known as prostate enlargement, this condition is mostly brought about by the aging process in dogs. BPH is not cancerous. When BPH happens, the prostate swells and crushes against the dog's rectum, causing discomfort. Without treatment, BPH causes bowel and bladder problems in the dog. The primary treatment for BPH is neutering.

Prostatitis is a bacterial infection of the prostate gland. The prostate becomes inflamed and tender. Signs of prostatitis include

- fever
- cloudy or bloody discharge from the penis
- blood in the urine
- abdominal discomfort
- stiff gait
- weakness
- lethargy
- straining to urinate or defecate
- anorexia
- vomiting

- weight loss
- chronic intermittent urinary tract infections

This can turn into a chronic condition, and chronic prostatitis is a significant factor behind canine male infertility.

Prostatitis is believed to be caused by an infection in the urethra but can also become infected from infections in the bladder, kidneys or blood. E. coli is the most common bacterium that causes infection.

Prostate cancer is a type of cancer rarely seen in dogs. However, prostate cancer is the most serious among the types of prostate problems in older dogs. Because this cancer type is not influenced in any way by testosterone, it can strike in both neutered and non-neutered dogs. As with most cancers, prostate cancer is a life-threatening condition, especially since surgery in removing the cancer cells is difficult due to the location of the affected region.

The treatment methods for prostate problems affecting dogs depend on the type of prostate problem and its severity. Veterinarians usually prescribe medications, like antibiotics, to control and reduce the swelling. For prostate cancer, surgery and chemotherapy are the usual treatments of choice, although most dog owners discover the cancer when it's already in its late stages.

Prevent prostate problems in older dogs from happening by providing your dog with a healthy lifestyle and taking him to the vet when you spot something suspicious.

Urinary Incontinence

Urinary incontinence is proof that humans and dogs aren't any different when it comes to growing old. Dogs also lose their voluntary ability to control their bladders as they approach their senior years. If you find your old house-trained pooch starting to seemingly relieve his bladder in random corners of the house, don't get angry with him. Your dog didn't merely stumble upon a new desire to suddenly soil your house. He is growing old, and the aging process is beginning to take its toll on your dog's bodily functions.

There are several factors that contribute to urinary incontinence in older dogs. One very common factor is the decreasing ability of the urethral muscles—which are primarily responsible for holding your dog's urine until your dog voluntarily decides to pee. As your dog grows older, the urethral muscles weaken, leading to your dog's inability to hold his pee as well as he did in his younger years. Weak urethral muscles sometimes cause your old dog to let go of urine even while he is sleeping.

In female dogs, the inability to keep and hold urine in the bladder is brought about by the decrease of estrogen levels. Urinary incontinence in older dogs, specifically in females, takes place when the urethra gradually loses its muscle tone. This loss of muscle tone is a result of the dipping estrogen levels, leading to the condition that is called spay incontinence.

Other underlying conditions can cause urinary incontinence. Conditions such as bladder problems (e.g., an infection) and neurologic illnesses (e.g., a disc rupture) are some of the known culprits behind a dog's sudden lack of control in his bladder-related activities. Other usual conditions that contribute to bladder problems in canines are diabetes and kidney disease. These conditions bring changes to your dog's body that causes him to produce more urine than usual. Couple diabetes/kidney issues with old age and your poor pooch really has a hard time holding her pee!

If you suspect your dog is suffering from urinary incontinence, take him to the vet. The vet will conduct exams and tests to check if the incontinence is either purely due to the loss of muscle tone in the urethra or due to the presence of an underlying disease.

The usual treatment for urinary incontinence in older dogs involves giving your pooch medications that can help increase the tone of his urethral muscles. If the incontinence is due to the presence of an illness or disease, the vet often deals with the illness first. Keeping the disease under control also helps keep your dog's bladder incontinence under control.

Chronic Valvular Disease

Chronic valvular disease in older dogs is a condition that takes place when degenerative changes occur in the mitral valve, which is situated between the left atrium and left ventricle in the heart. The heart's tricuspid valve may also be affected, but this event rarely happens. These degenerative changes build up and become stronger over time, leading to chronic changes in your dog's heart function and, unless medical attention is given, heart failure.

There is no known cause for chronic valvular disease; it seems to be a bi-product of the aging process. Simply said, the normally sharp edges of the heart valves become thick and stiff, hence taking on a distorted appearance. Because of these abnormal changes, the heart valves can't close completely and properly. This causes an abnormal flow of blood in the heart.

Chronic valvular disease affects more than 35 percent of dogs over 12 years old. In general, the disease is seen in 20-40% of canines; particularly in small-breed and toy dogs. Chronic valvular disease in older dogs is dominant in breeds such as

- Cocker Spaniel
- Chihuahua
- Schnauzer
- Toy and Miniature Poodles
- Yorkshire Terrier

In most cases, dog owners become aware of the presence of chronic valvular disease in their pooches only during the later stages. By then the damage is done, and sometimes, it can even be fatal. To prevent this from happening to you and your dog, look out for these early signs of chronic valvular disease:

- Post-exercise or nightly coughing
- Exercise intolerance
- Lethargy
- Fainting spells

The primary indication of chronic valvular disease in older dogs is the presence of a loud heart murmur that is located and heard usually at the left side of your pooch's chest. The murmur becomes louder as the disease progresses and worsens.

Chronic valvular disease is incurable, but with early detection and prompt medical treatment, its progression can be managed and controlled. If you suspect your old dog has chronic valvular disease, bring him to the vet immediately for tests and diagnostic procedures. The vet will conduct a physical examination, take blood samples, and use radiographs to determine if your dog indeed has the disease. The procedure may also include an ultrasound and EKG.

Chronic valvular disease in older dogs is kept under control with medications aimed to help the heart perform its function. Modifications in your dog's diet and exercise programs are other treatment methods. Note that the treatment plan depends on certain factors, such as the severity of the disease.

You can't prevent your old dog from getting chronic valvular disease. But with a healthy lifestyle, nutritious diet, and early intervention, your old dog can live comfortably with the disease.

Cardiomyopathy

The heart is one of the most hardworking organs in both the human and canine body. And whether its man or man's best friend, age-related factors can cause heart conditions. Along with chronic valvular disease and heartworm, cardiomyopathy is one of the common types of heart disease affecting the canine world.

In simple terms, cardiomyopathy brings about the enlargement of the walls of the four chambers of the heart. This enlargement makes it difficult for the heart to perform its pumping motion effectively. Also, the valves of the heart become leaky.

While cardiomyopathy is seen in both the left and right side of the heart, one side is usually more seriously affected than the other. The heart is divided into the upper chamber (atria) and lower chamber (ventricle). Upon deterioration of the cardiac muscle both the upper and lower chambers enlarge. The ventricles become weak; hence their ability to pump blood becomes impaired. As a result, instead of circulating smoothly all over the body, blood pools in the dog's body and fluid sometimes drops back into the abdomen, lungs, and other body parts.

Cardiomyopathy is a disease that moves silently. Signs and symptoms show up when the disease is in the later stages, which is often too late for your dog. The disease commonly affects larger breeds. These breeds include the Doberman Pinscher, Boxer, Great Dane, Saint Bernard, Retrievers (Golden and Labs) and Irish Wolfhound. Experts believe the disease has a genetic trigger, although the actual cause has yet to be determined.

If your pooch is genetically predisposed to cardiomyopathy, here are the signs you need to look out for:

- Labored breathing
- Lethargy or fatigue
- Decreased appetite
- Coughing

Cardiomyopathy in older dogs is the most common reason for congestive heart failure in canines. Watch out for these signs, which indicate heart failure:

- Loss of consciousness
- Tongue turns blue
- Rapid breathing
- Excessive drooling

If your dog exhibits any of the signs above, take him to the vet *immediately*. Your dog is likely experiencing heart failure, and failure to act right away could lead to fatal results.

Your vet can detect cardiomyopathy in your pooch before it's too late through regular health checkups. Once confirmed, cardiomyopathy in older dogs is usually treated using cardiac medications, such as digitalis. This is to facilitate heart function. You may also need to change your dog's diet to a low-sodium diet. There are low-sodium commercial dog foods available with a vet's prescription.

Some studies, particularly with the Boxer breed, suggest that cardiomyopathy may be the result of a deficiency in an amino acid called L-carnitine. If this turns out to be the cause of your dog's heart problem, the treatment may be supplementing the diet with carnitine.

If your vet diagnoses the problem early, it is not uncommon for dogs to live for two more years. However, a late diagnosis generally results in a pet passing with a year, and possibly within a couple of weeks.

Hypothyroidism

Hypothyroidism is the most common endocrine disorder in older dogs. This condition impacts the thyroid gland. The thyroid gland is a tiny gland that sits in the neck region, near what people call the Adam's apple. The gland has two lobes, which can be felt through palpation.

The primary role of the thyroid gland is to convert iodine into triiodothyronine (T3) and thyroxine (T4), the two major thyroid hormones. These hormones circulate throughout the body and affect every cell metabolism.

The thyroid gland pumps out just the right amount of T3 and T4, thanks to the thyroid stimulating hormone (TSH) released by the hypothalamus and pituitary glands. With this feedback mechanism, dogs get the right amount of thyroid hormones in their bodies.

Hypothyroidism occurs in older dogs when this feedback mechanism is disrupted. As a result of this disruption, production and secretion of the thyroid hormones decrease.

The causes of hypothyroidism in canines fall into one of two categories:

- **Primary hypothyroidism** is the most common cause for canine cases and it occurs because the dog's body produces antibodies against the thyroid gland, eventually destroying it. (Lymphocytic thyroiditis)

- **Secondary hypothyroidism** occurs when there is too little TSH, or because of disease and medication. Cases of hypothyroidism in older dogs because of secondary reasons are rare.

Since the thyroid hormones travel throughout the body, it's tough to diagnose hypothyroidism. Nevertheless, here are the signs you should look out for in your pooch:
- Lethargy
- Unexplained weight gain
- Intolerance to physical activity
- Hair loss
- Skin infection

- Heat-seeking actions (e.g., your old dog searches for warm areas to lie down)

Aside from your dog's age, one factor that comes into play with your dog's susceptibility to hypothyroidism is his breed. These breeds are more prone to the disease than others:

- Akita
- American Cocker Spaniel
- Beagle
- Boxer
- Doberman Pinscher
- German Shepherd
- Golden Retriever
- Great Dane
- Rottweiler

The good news is that hypothyroidism in older dogs is treatable. After the vet performs a series of tests to confirm your dog has hypothyroidism, he'll likely be prescribed thyroid supplements. These supplements are in pill form which are to be given to your dog for the rest of his life.

It's important to monitor your old dog's condition even when he is taking medication. Keep an eye out for possible adverse reactions to the prescribed medicines, a sudden appearance of another sign indicating hypothyroidism in older dogs, or a worsening of any of the already existing symptoms. If you spot any change in your old dog, contact your vet right away.

Cushing's Disease

Cushing's disease is a condition that mimics the natural aging process of the canine body. But don't fall into the trap of thinking the things your dog is going through are simply due to age. Cushing's disease is a malady common in older dogs. While the signs are hard to spot, the disorder is manageable and can be controlled as long as it is detected in your dog early enough.

Cushing's disease is medically known as hyperadrenocorticism. It is a disorder of the endocrine system and occurs when the negative feedback loop normally present in healthy dogs suddenly gets out of whack. Hormones are secreted improperly and in incorrect amounts, throwing the entire system off.

In Cushing's disease, the pituitary gland produces excessive amounts of the adrenocorticotrophic hormone (ACTH). This hormone triggers the adrenal glands to produce steroid hormones, one of which is cortisol. Since the pituitary gland secretes too much ACTH, the adrenal glands, in turn, give off too much cortisol. As a result, the dog's system is overflowing and being poisoned with cortisol.

Tumors (either a pituitary brain tumor or an adrenal gland tumor) are the most common cause for this disease which throws the dog's feedback loop off track. There is no particular reason for the appearance of tumors, except for the fact that dogs are likely to get them as they grow older. Also, Cushing's disease affects female dogs more than males by a 60/40 margin.

Cushing's disease presents telltale signs that are tricky and vague to figure out. Look out for these common symptoms:

- Increased water intake
- Increased appetite
- Frequent urination
- Muscle weakness
- Bulging or bloated abdomen
- Hair loss
- Skin lumps
- Thin, wrinkled skin

You may have noticed the signs above are similar to other canine diseases and conditions. A dead giveaway of Cushing's disease, though, is the presence of a bulging or bloated belly, in large part due to the decline in muscle strength and fat redistribution from the other parts of the body to the abdomen.

If you suspect your beloved companion has Cushing's disease, bring him to the vet immediately. The vet will perform a series of tests and procedures to determine if your dog indeed has the condition. Treatment for Cushing's disease in older dogs largely involves drug therapy. Mitotane, trilostane, ketoconazole, and L-Deprenyl hydrochloride are popular choices. Each has its own side effect, though, so always ask your vet which is the best choice for your furry friend.

If left untreated, Cushing's disease can lead to even more serious health problems down the road. These include heart disease, diabetes, kidney failure, and chronic infections, such as those of the skin.

With early intervention though Cushing's disease in older dogs can be kept under control for many, many years and your pup can continue to live a good, quality life.

For more information on Cushing's disease, visit: www.vetinfo.com/dcushing2.html

Kidney Disease

Kidney disease, also known as renal failure, occurs when a dog's kidneys are no longer able to get rid of the harmful substances in the bloodstream and regulate blood pressure, blood volume, body fluids, and hormones. Although it can strike in dogs of any age, kidney disease is more frequent in older dogs.

Kidney disease can be either acute or chronic. Acute kidney disease, as the name implies, occurs rapidly and without warning. The kidneys suddenly cease to perform their functions of fluid regulation and waste elimination. Note that this is an <u>emergency situation</u>. Failure of the kidneys to carry out their tasks can result to a sharp increase in blood pressure, heart failure, and, if medical attention isn't given to the dog, death.

Chronic kidney failure occurs more slowly—so slowly, in fact, that by the time the symptoms begin to appear, the disease is usually on its advanced stages. Kidney disease in older dogs cannot be cured effectively if discovered too late. Unfortunately, this is more often the case for most older dogs.

Kidney disease is best fought during its early stages. For this to be possible, you need to keep a watchful eye on your older dog should he exhibit any of the following signs indicating kidney disease:

- Increased water intake
- Frequent urination
- Vomiting
- Diarrhea
- Lethargy
- Weight loss
- Decreased appetite
- Blood in urine
- Depression

Certain breeds of dogs appear to be predisposed to kidney disease, including:

- Bull Terrier
- Cairn Terrier
- English Cocker Spaniel
- German Shepherd

- Doberman Pinscher
- Samoyed
- Shar–pei

Kidney disease in older dogs is brought about by many factors. Age, infection (bacterial, viral, or fungal), inflammation, cancer, autoimmune disease, toxicity, and parasites are some of the factors that come into play. Sometimes, acute kidney disease develops into a chronic condition over time.

A dysfunction of the other body organs is another cause of kidney disease. For example, a problem in a dog's heart affects the blood flow from the heart to the kidneys. This decrease in blood flow hampers the kidney's ability to function, potentially leading to the disease.

Kidney disease, particularly the chronic type, has no cure. The focus of treatment for kidney disease in older dogs is to keep the illness under control, minimize symptoms, and slow down its progression. Treatment methods include a special vet-approved diet that's low in sodium, protein, and calcium; keeping your dog hydrated at all times by providing him clean and fresh drinking water; and giving vet-approved supplements to help boost your dog's appetite.

Living with a dog that has kidney disease requires constant monitoring and regular checkups to the vet to make sure your dog's condition remains stable. Kidney disease is a progressive disease; hence, it will be with your dog for as long as he lives. With proper treatment, kidney disease won't prevent your dog from enjoying a normal, fun-filled life.

Glaucoma

Glaucoma is "a disease of the eye marked by increased pressure within the eyeball that can result in damage to the optic disk and gradual loss of vision." The disease acts and progresses swiftly, and unless immediate medical attention is given, your old dog's eyesight can be lost in only a matter of days. Hence, glaucoma in older dogs is a situation that can be classified as a medical emergency.

There are two types of glaucoma:

Primary glaucoma can be due to congenital causes or the dog is genetically predisposed to the disease. Some breeds that have a genetic disposition for glaucoma are

- Basset Hounds
- Poodles
- Beagles

This type of glaucoma appears without any insult or injury to the eye.

Secondary glaucoma has nothing to do with genetics and can affect any breed. This type of glaucoma usually stems from another disease in the eye, such as lens dislocation or tumors within the eye.

The specific cause behind glaucoma in older dogs and even in their younger counterparts is currently unknown. Studies confirm that the disease often appears suddenly and without warning. Experts also have yet to understand why glaucoma usually occurs in the later stages of a dog's life.

Glaucoma is a sneaky disease. It doesn't show signs until the advanced stages, and by then, it's too late to do anything. Here are the signs to watch out for:
- Redness in the eye
- Squinting
- Tearing up
- Sensitivity to light
- Cloudy or hazy appearance

If you spot these signs of glaucoma in older dogs, especially if your pooch is of a breed that's genetically predisposed to glaucoma, take your furry friend to the vet immediately. This quick response can save your dog's vision.

While there is no specific cure for glaucoma, early medical intervention makes a huge difference in preventing your old dog from going blind. In the early stages of the disease, non-invasive procedures are applied. Vets often prescribe eye drops and oral medication for old dogs afflicted with glaucoma. Glaucoma is a lifelong condition, so you need to administer medication to your pooch for the rest of his life.

Surgery is another option for treating glaucoma. Laser surgery works just as well in dogs as it does in humans. In rare events, the dog's affected eye is removed, and a glass or prosthetic eye is put in its place. This procedure is done for aesthetic reasons.

Cataracts

The formation of cataracts is one of the most common eye problems in dogs. The American College of Veterinary Ophthalmologists reports that cataracts are believed to be inherited in ninety-seven breeds, although fifteen additional breeds have been confirmed to suffer from cataracts through inheritance. Cataracts are more common in older dogs than in younger pets. Still, regardless of age, any dog is at risk of forming cataracts.

To understand how cataracts form, first we need to understand the anatomy of the eye. One part of the eye is the lens. The lens, a transparent material, is located at the back of the pupil. It's the lens that focuses and directs light into the retina, which then transmits the image to the brain. The brain is where vision is actually perceived.

Cataract formation takes place when the cells and proteins that make up the lens start to degenerate. This degeneration causes the lens to be cloudy. When the lens gets clouded up, light cannot be focused on the retina and vision is then affected.

According to Animal Eye Care in Bellingham, Washington, there are several causes of cataracts in dogs. Dr. Terri McCalla explains the various causes in order from the most common to the least common:

- *Most cataracts in dogs are inherited and may develop rapidly over weeks, or slowly over years, and occur in one or both eyes.*
- *The second-most common cause of cataracts in dogs is diabetes. 75% of diabetic dogs will develop blinding cataracts within the first year of being diabetic. Diabetic cataracts develop VERY fast—often overnight—in dogs, and they are a medical and surgical emergency.*
- *The third most common cause of cataracts in dogs is called "toxic cataracts". Toxic cataracts caused by ocular disease are quite common in dogs, and are caused by: 1) retinal degeneration 2) uveitis (intraocular inflammation) of any cause, including trauma; and 3) secondary to glaucoma (increased intraocular pressure) of any cause.*
- *A special type of cataract occurs in dogs in which the lens capsule is ruptured due to trauma. It is not always apparent that the lens capsule has ruptured; often, by the time this is diagnosed it is too late to save the eye and the eye needs to be removed. Thus, it is prudent to*

> seek immediate medical attention for ANY injury to your dog's eye.
- *Dogs also can develop cataracts with age (often after 8 years of life). However, age-related cataracts in dogs are usually small and do not significantly interfere with vision.*

So how do you spot a cataract? Take a close look at your dog's eyes. A slight hazy appearance on one or both of his pupils is a normal event that comes with growing old. This appearance has an almost-negligible, if any, effect on your dog's vision, so don't panic if this hazy look is present in your dog. However, if the pupils appear milky and seem to bear a resemblance to crushed ice—even if it only shows in a single pupil—make an appointment with your vet right away. Another telltale sign your pooch has a cataract is when he doesn't seem to see as well or as clearly as he used to.

Cataract treatment in older dogs is similar to cataract treatment in people wherein a surgeon removes the lens from the affected eye and replaces it with a synthetic one. Although surgical procedures for removing cataracts in dogs have high success rates, it's still best to find a surgeon who has considerable experience to further improve your dog's chance of success.

Some of the breeds that have a high propensity for forming cataracts are:
- American Cocker Spaniel
- Bichon Frise
- Boston Terrier
- Havanese
- Miniature Schnauzer
- Silky Terrier
- Smooth Fox Terrier
- Toy Poodle

Arthritis

Arthritis means "degeneration of a joint" in the literal sense. Any injury to the joint has the potential to result in arthritis later on. Arthritis refers to the "inflammation of joints due to infectious, metabolic, or constitutional causes." Some common causes of arthritis:

- Disease of the ligament, muscle, or tendon (e.g., a tear in the anterior cruciate ligament)
- Developmental disorders (e.g., hip dysplasia)
- Joint fractures
- Inflammatory joint disease (e.g., rheumatoid arthritis)
- Congenital disorders (e.g., luxated patella)

Similar to humans, arthritis in an older dog is very common. In fact, one-out-of-every-five dogs over the age of seven suffers from Arthritis.

According to America's Largest Pet Pharmacy, 1800PetMeds, "Most dogs in their senior years have arthritis. In fact, osteoarthritis (OA) is the most common skeletal disease of dogs. Working, athletic, obese dogs-and those with diabetes or Cushing's disease-are especially prone. Trauma and injury, hip dysplasia or elbow dysplasia also predispose pets to arthritis."

Arthritis in an older dog isn't immediately visible to the naked eye. But once you take a closer look at your pooch, you'll notice there's suddenly something wrong with the way he walks or the way he gets up from his favorite resting position. Stiffness and lameness are often the first signs of arthritis, but along with these two, other signs may crop up as well. Signs your old dog could have arthritis include:
- Depression
- Lethargy
- Decreased appetite
- Deformed and swollen joints
- Irritability
- Exercise intolerance

Arthritis is a progressive condition. Hence, the signs appear mild or almost nonexistent at first, only becoming more obvious as the disease progresses.

Arthritis in an older dog is difficult to determine without the help of diagnostic tests and measures. Sometimes, the signs are confused as being part of the aging process. Some pet owners think their furry friends are depressed or lethargic because their canine buddies are growing old. If you notice something odd in your older dog, call the vet and describe what you're noticing. The vet will likely ask you to bring your old pooch in for a checkup.

While there isn't a cure for arthritis, there are several ways to manage the pain and discomfort that come with the disease. The vet is likely to prescribe painkillers and supplements for your older dog. More ways to reduce the unpleasant effects of arthritis in your older dog are:

Manage your dog's weight. If your old dog is overweight, the excess weight adds strain to his inflamed joins. Ridding him of those extra pounds will make him feel better.

Get your dog moving. Exercise is good for dogs of all shapes and ages—yes, even an old dog with arthritis. Swimming is the best exercise for a dog with arthritis because it has low impact on the joints. You might consider taking your dog to an indoor canine swimming center. Walking is also good for arthritic dogs. Constant motion prevents the joints from getting stiff, so be sure your dog gets to exercise often.

Make the necessary modifications. With his joints in pain, not all activities are going to be a pleasant experience for your dog. Arthritis makes doing normal, everyday activities a challenge for your pet. In this case, modify. Make use of ramps instead of stairs. Elevate your dog's food and water bowls. Make sure her bed is thick and soft.

Your old dog can live a quality life with arthritis. But it will definitely be better for her with the correct medications, weight control, exercise and modifications.

Many breeds are predisposed to arthritis.

American Bulldog
American Staffordshire Terrier
Beagle
Bernese Mountain Dog
Bloodhound
Bouvier des Flandres
Golden Retriever
Gordon Setter
Irish Water Spaniel
Kuvasz
Neapolitan Mastiff
Newfoundland
Norwegian Elkhound

Boykin Spaniel
Briard
Brittany
Bulldog
Bullmastiff
Chesapeake Bay Retriever
Chow Chow
Clumber Spaniel
Coonhound (Black and Tan)
Coton de Tuléar
Curly Coated Retriever
English Setter
English Springer Spaniel
German Shepherd
Giant Schnauzer

Old English Sheepdog
Otterhund
Polish Lowland Sheepdog
Portuguese Water Dog
Pudel Pointer
Pug
Rottweiler
Shih Tzu
Spanish Water Dog
St. Bernard
Staffordshire Terrier
Sussex Spaniel
Welsh Corgi
Welsh Springer Spaniel

Dental Disease and Gingivitis

Dental disease and gingivitis in an older dog is a widespread yet treatable health problem. Dental disease in canines is a generic term that refers to "a progression of disease that affects multiple structures within the oral cavity or mouth." Common names of this condition are dental disease and cavities, while its scientific names are periodontitis and gingivitis.

Regardless of age, dental disease is one of the most common problems plaguing dogs. According to studies, roughly 80% of dogs will form some degree of dental problems when they are 3-4 years old. Dental disease begins with plaque and tartar. When left untreated, this leads to gingivitis, an "inflammation of the gums that is often accompanied by tenderness and bleeding" and is the earliest sign of periodontal disease.

Periodontal disease is the final result of dental disease and gingivitis in an older dog. This is when the structures that support and keep the teeth in place become diseased. In the final stages of periodontal disease, tooth loss occurs.

Halitosis, or bad breath, is the first sign of dental disease. If you find yourself grimacing in disgust every time you get a whiff of your old dog's breath, that's a red flag. Other early signs are red, swollen gums that have begun to recede, drooling, inability to hold food due to pain, and a colored discharge from the nostrils. Another sign may include swelling in the area between the mouth and eye.

Dental disease affects the organ systems in dogs. Other than the mouth, the bone, muscles, and tissues lodged beneath the skin can also be affected by the condition.

Dental disease and gingivitis in your older dog can be prevented. Experts agree that the most effective combat against the disease is regular, thorough brushing of your dog's teeth, a habit that is best begun in puppyhood. Use cleaning products specifically made for pets. **Never use toothpaste made for humans** as it has fluoride, a substance that is toxic to pets when ingested.

In addition to regular brushing by you, be sure to get professional care through routine prophylaxis or cleanings by the Vet. During these oral care visits, the vet will conduct screenings and tests to probe in your dog's mouth so oral problems, if any, can be detected right away.

Battling dental disease and gingivitis in your older dog can be made fun by giving your dog some chew treats. These help scrub away the tartar buildup on your dog's teeth. You can also ask your vet for specialized food that can reduce plaque and tartar buildup. Oral antibacterial solutions are also available. You can squirt the solution onto your dog's teeth to reduce buildup.

Proper oral care takes time and effort, but it staves off dental disease and gingivitis in your older dog. After all, a healthy mouth means a healthy dog.

CPSIA information can be obtained at www.ICGtesting.com
Printed in the USA
BVOW08s1319180115

383813BV00019B/1005/P